I0155450

YOU CAN'T
SERVE
2 MASTERS

A GUIDE FOR EFFECTIVE DECISION MAKING

Copyright © 2024 by Davielier E. Turner

All rights reserved.

No part of this book may be reproduced in any form or by any electronic or mechanical means, including information storage and retrieval systems, without written permission from the author, except for the use of brief quotations in a book review.

YOU CAN'T
SERVE
2 MASTERS

A GUIDE FOR EFFECTIVE DECISION MAKING

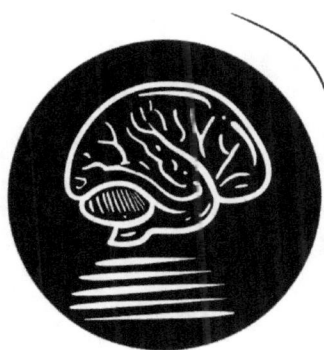

DAVIELIER E. TURNER

CONTENTS

This book is dedicated to the people that my decisions has been based on the last three decades of my life. This book is dedicated to Rasheda Turner my daughter Destinee and my two grandchildren Mason & Meadow. Life is never easy, and decisions are even harder. The key to life is to always try to make the best decisions possible. We must remember that our decisions do not only affect us but the family that we have created. Always remember to try your best and always give your all because there is always a win in those things. There is no such thing as failure as long if you know that you made the right decision for yourself.

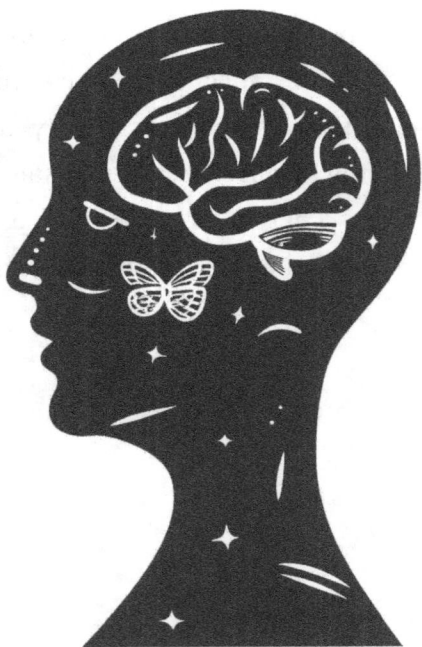

Are you having trouble making the correct decisions in life, business and in general. We know it gets hard but when you clamp down to serve one side then and only then life becomes easier. Is it choices, decisions, thoughts, second guessing or anything that makes the decision harder. In this book we will get to the point that helps make the right decision with effective decision making.

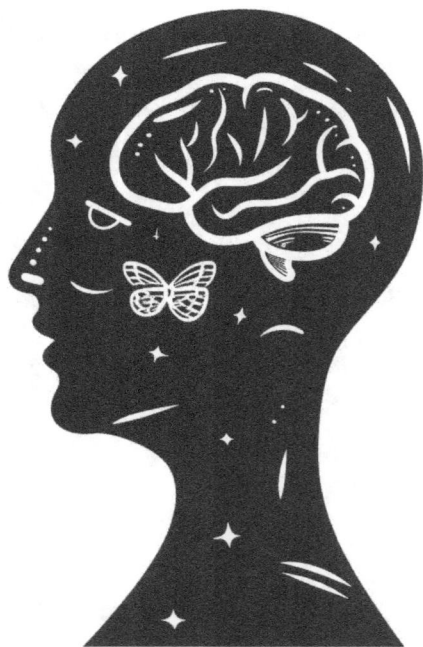

INTRODUCTION

"You Can't Serve 2 Masters: The Art of Affective Decision Making" is a thought-provoking book that delves into the complexities of decision-making and the impact of emotions on our choices. Drawing from psychology, neuroscience, and personal anecdotes, this book explores the concept of affective decision making and provides practical strategies to make more effective and fulfilling decisions.

The book begins by examining the common dilemma of trying to please everyone and the detrimental effects it can have on our decision-making process. It highlights the importance of understanding our own values, desires, and priorities in order to make decisions that align with our authentic selves.

Through engaging stories and insightful analysis, the author illustrates the power of emotions in decision making. It explores how our emotions can influence our perceptions, biases, and reasoning abilities, and provides guidance on how to navigate these influences to make more rational and balanced choices.

"You Can't Serve 2 Masters" also addresses the challenges of decision-making in a fast-paced and complex world. It offers strategies to manage information overload, deal with uncertainty, and overcome decision paralysis. The book emphasizes the significance of mindfulness and self-awareness in the decision-making process, encouraging readers to tap into their intuition and inner wisdom.

Furthermore, the book explores the impact of decision-making on our overall well-being and relationships. It delves into the consequences of making decisions that go against our values or neglect our emotional needs and provides insights on how to align our choices with our long-term happiness and fulfillment.

In conclusion, "You Can't Serve 2 Masters: The Art of Affective Decision Making" is a compelling guide that challenges conventional wisdom and provides a fresh perspective on decision-making. It equips readers with the tools and insights needed to make more authentic, balanced, and fulfilling choices in all aspects of life. Whether you are facing major life decisions or simply seeking to improve your everyday decision-making, this book will inspire and empower you to embrace the art of affective decision making.

"In any moment of decision, the best thing you can do is the right thing, the next best thing is the wrong thing, and the worst thing you can do is nothing."

—Theodore Roosevelt

ONE

WANTING TO DO RIGHT

On the day we are born we are born just innocent and pure in the image of our parents and the god of your understanding. Nothing bothers us, the world is just a canvas for us to create on once we first open our eyes. There is nothing but hugs, blurry faces and people speaking with funny noises such as goo goo gaa gaa and just mumbling gibberish. Everyone wants to smell you, hold you and rock you. The world is at your feet for the moment. Life is simple and life is plain. Our innocence is there, and we enjoy it because we do not know the way of the world just yet.

As a child we often heard our parents say do the right thing, make the right choices, make us proud. When we heard this, it made us try to give our all to make them happy and proud, we started living to please them because life was easy then. The cares of the world were minimal there was no stress and no pressure on any of our backs to do anything as a child but be a good child. Life was so simple and easy then, they made all the choices for us from food to clothes, to games and all. The picked the schools, haircuts/ hairstyles the lunch we ate and gave us a kiss before leaving for class. Life was easy and life was great. This went on for a few years but what was it that exposed us to thinking different about the choices and the decisions that we should make in life? Was it just the idea of getting older? Was it the school itself? Was it the peers in the school that we saw acting different and we wanted to just see what it felt like for just that first time? As we got older, we started changing, decisions were different, choices were difficult, and we started comparing things that were once simplified. The older we turned the more confusing this has gotten because we started to understand and see that there were two sides of a coin. Good & bad, right, or wrong, left or right, up or down, love or hate, success or failure and the simple things became difficult to us. There was no straight path anymore it was like how did all this change so suddenly, where did all these choices come from and what should I do? Should I go left, right, front, back, top or bottom and once that happens it becomes so much easier to make the wrong choice very quickly. We all want to do right. Everyone in the world at one time wanted to do right, or did they? Choices is no easy task as well as deciding to make the right choice at the right time. Everyday life and its decisions get even more difficult. A decision with your back against the wall and in debt is a different decision from when all your bills are paid, and you have a substantial amount of money saved in the bank. A Homeless man decision is way different than the CEO of a fortune 500 company, because of the circumstances of their being, but they're both one choice from being in the same boat either way. So, wanting to do right and doing right is a matter of what situation in life you're in at this present day and time.

I know it seem like we all speak as if this is just black and white and oh so simple. Is it really? Look at the world around us, the people around us and some of the decisions that we have made compared to the decisions that's some of our family members and peers have made. Now ask yourself again. Is it all so simple or is it harder for some than it is for others or is it just a matter of decisions that one made at an earlier point in their life. Truth of the matters is there is no real logical answer, and the answer can come down to one's decisions either right or wrong and that can be right for the moment or wrong for the moment. The decision is yours and only yours to make.

"One seldom recognizes the devil when he is putting his hand on your shoulder."

—Albert Speer

TWO

DEVIL ON YOUR SHOULDER

Remember back in the day we would see the cartoons and every time they had to make a rational decision you would see an angel on one of the shoulders and the devil with his fork on the other shoulder. The angel and the devil were just symbolic to how you make the right and wrong choice. The angel would always shake his head and just say do it this way and don't listen to him, but the devil's energy was always hyper and telling them to do it another way and make the other decision.

This is how life is because two different decisions will really have two different outcomes on your life, your success, your family, your hope and dreams, your goals and your future. But one decision must be made and that is the path one will walk once that decision is made.

When I say the devil is on my shoulder, I really mean it! I haven't always been this professional and have made some very bad decisions in my life that encountered bad results. But the truth is that's what taught me valuable lessons on why I should choose right instead of wrong, left instead of right, or right instead of left.

The hardest part is always doing right because there is always a short cut to get there we believe, but every shortcut is not a shortcut. Some are blocked roadways and mental blocks to slow down your progress. There is no shortcut to success. One must do the work that it requires in order to really be successful. As a licensed Real Estate broker and Licensed Real estate instructor there are no shortcuts to getting these Certifications, you must put the time in and have the experience before you can even take the broker's test. Then you must wait a specific time before you can even take the instructor's test. I tried to take a shortcut on the instructors test my first time, but it didn't work so I failed and honestly, I never failed any of my exams I passed all of them on the first try. But here I go with the angel and devil on my shoulder again. The angel saying study everything the devil saying just study the real estate part of the test you will pass you have over 20 years in real estate. I did that and failed but this was another life lesson that there are no shortcuts in life. The Real Estate commission had referred a book to me called "Teaching to Adults" to study before I took my instructor exam, and I didn't read it. Once I failed that day I went home and only read that book for three days straight no television, no radio, no disruptions because failing did not sit good within myself. My desire wouldn't let me accept that defeat mentally. So, I stayed up and studied, studied, and then studied some more for three straight days. The fourth day I went back to take the new Jersey State Real Estate Instructor exam again and I had passed it. Although I had passed, I had also lost because I tried to take a shortcut by listening to the devil on my shoulder. I lost three whole days to studying that I could have used the energy elsewhere. I lost another $60 because I had to repay to take the test again. Time I will never get back I lost three days of my life because I didn't want to do it the right way the first time. I let the devil on my shoulder convince me that I knew enough and then when I went back to the angel, I had finally passed the exam. But that's right or wrong, wrong, or right and the doing things right the first time so that way you do not have to double back and lose time by having to do it over again.

That was a lesson learned and like I said there is always an Angel and devil because I should have known better this wasn't my first rodeo dealing with either of them. Yet Somehow, we know it's wrong but still try to take the road with less steps when if we take the road with correct way of doing things it's easier. I might not seem like it but doing the same thing twice does not sound like a shortcut to me when it could have been done right the first time. There are no shortcuts to success.

Sometimes, we all face an internal struggle between what we know is right and the tempting allure of the easier, but morally questionable path. It's as if a devil sits on our shoulder, whispering per- suasively, clouding our judgment. In these moments, it's crucial to acknowledge the source of this negative influence and confront it head-on.

Identifying the reasons behind the devil's influence is the first step. Are external pressures, personal desires, or fear guiding this influence? Understanding the root cause can help you address the issue more effectively.

Moreover, surrounding yourself with positive influences and supportive individuals can create a counterbalance to the devil's whispers. Seek guidance from those who share your values and can offer a different perspective on the situation. Sometimes, a fresh outlook can help you see the right path more clearly.

Remember, the devil on your shoulder may be persistent, but your internal compass can guide you toward making the right choices. Reflect on your values, consider the potential consequences of your actions, and strive to align your decisions with the person you aspire to be. In overcoming this internal struggle, you'll not only do the right thing but also strengthen your resilience against future temptations.

I have an Angel on one shoulder and the devil on the other. I'm also def in on ear.

—"Unknown"

THREE

GOOD ME VS BAD ME

I never really used to believe in the horoscope stuff and the signs until I turned older and as a Gemini sign, I can really say that there is a good me and it is always fiercely battling the bad me. It's a game of tug-war sometimes and both sides are pretty much "even" if you let me tell it.

But by me understanding and compressing my thoughts words and actions is what really makes a difference in the battle of Me's. Let me explain further.

Within each of us, there exists a complex inter-play between the good and the bad aspects of our character. The "good" in me represents the qualities that bring out the best in my interactions with the world. It encompasses compassion, empathy, kind-ness, and the desire to make a positive impact. This facet of my personality drives me to help others, to be understanding in times of conflict, and to seek per-sonal growth through self-improvement and learn-ing. It's the part of me that strives to create harmony and leave a lasting, positive mark on the people and places I encounter. It's sort of my what will they re-member about you statement.

On the other hand, the "bad" in me comprises the less favorable aspects of my character, including moments of selfishness, impatience, and negative emotions like anger or envy. Like I said before I am a Gemini sign so there is always some shady in me. It's a part of me that I acknowledge and, at times, strug-gle with. The "bad" in me serves as a reminder of my imperfections and the areas where I need to grow and evolve. While these qualities can sometimes lead to mistakes or regrets, they also offer opportunities for introspection and self-improvement of myself. This side helps me know that I am still a work in progress.

In the end, the dynamic interplay between the "good" and the "bad" within us is what makes us human. It's our responsibility to foster the positive aspects of our character and work on taming the negative ones. Acknowledging both sides allow us to develop self-awareness, resilience, and the capacity for personal transformation. This ongoing journey to balance the good and the bad is an essential part of the human experience, helping us grow into more compassionate, understanding, and better individuals.

That's why we must make sure that the good inside of us is way more dominant than the bad inside of us. If we strive to do right by people, help when we can, understand that the world might revolve around us, but it cannot revolve with missing and impure parts. When we plant generosity, love, peace and harmony in our hearts then the good us can always hold off the bad us from taking over the projection of us.

Opportunity never sneaks up on those who straddle the fence of **indecision**.

—Napoleon Hill.

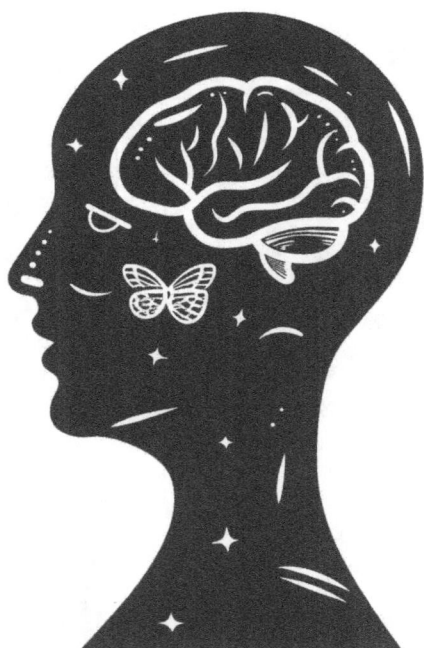

FOUR

STRADDLING THE FENCE

S traddling the fence between doing what's right and what is wrong is a precarious balancing act that many individuals find themselves engaged in at various points in their lives. This internal conflict often arises from ethical dilemmas, moral ambiguity, or the pressure of conflicting interests. At times, the line between right and wrong may appear blurred, making it challenging for individuals to make clear-cut decisions.

In such situations, individuals may grapple with their values and principles, torn between the desire to uphold moral standards and the temptation to take an easier, morally questionable path. The fear of consequences and the lure of short-term gains can contribute to the struggle of straddling the fence. This indecision may lead to internal turmoil, as individuals grapple with the consequences of their actions on both a personal and societal level.

Straddling the fence can also be a coping mechanism for those who fear the repercussions of taking a firm stance. The fear of alienation or backlash can drive individuals to remain on the fence, avoiding commitment to either side. This, however, comes at the cost of personal integrity, as avoiding a decision often means neglecting one's values and beliefs.

Moreover, societal, and cultural influences can exacerbate the challenge of straddling the fence. The pressure to conform to societal expectations or adhere to cultural norms may conflict with one's personal sense of morality. Navigating these external influences while trying to discern right from wrong adds another layer of complexity to the decision-making process.

Despite the difficulties, straddling the fence is not a sustainable or fulfilling long-term strategy. It can lead to internal turmoil, erode trust in relationships, and hinder personal growth. Ultimately, making choices aligned with one's values, even when it involves difficult decisions, is crucial for maintaining integrity and fostering a sense of self-worth.

The act of straddling the fence between doing what's right and what is wrong is a complex and challenging dilemma. It requires individuals to confront their values, navigate external pressures, and weigh the consequences of their actions. While the temptation to remain indecisive may be strong, embracing a commitment to ethical behavior is essential for personal growth and maintaining one's integrity in the face of moral ambiguity.

Straddling the fence also show a stance of lack of confidence in one's decision making. People that's 100% confidant do not straddle the fence they make the decision and leave it there, but a person that is not confident will stand there straddling the fence second guessing. Now don't get me wrong, I'm not saying don't second guess what I'm suggesting is to not over think and make a project out of the decision-making process. Build your yourself up to where you are very confident with your decision making.

"Your life changes the moment you make a new, congruent, and committed decision."

—Tony Robbins

FIVE

THE COMPLEXITY OF DECISION MAKING:

Navigating the complexities of decision-making is an intricate process that involves a myriad of factors. Firstly, decisions often require a deep understanding of the available information. This involves gathering relevant data, considering various perspectives, and acknowledging potential consequences. The volume and diversity of information available in the modern world can make this initial step particularly challenging, as individuals are often faced with an overwhelming amount of data to sift through.

Secondly, emotions play a significant role in decision-making. Human beings are inherently emotional creatures, and these emotions can influence choices both positively and negatively. Striking the right balance between logical reasoning and emotional intelligence is crucial. Embracing emotions can provide valuable insights, but unchecked emotional responses may cloud judgment. The challenge lies in recognizing and managing these emotions to arrive at decisions that align with both rational thinking and emotional well-being. For example, breaking up in a relationship can have a different effect based on where you are at emotionally. If you break up and you are not too involved or vested your emotions might not really care, but if you break up and you believe that you gave your all every day, every night then went above and beyond the relationship can play on your emotions differently. Your inner emotions can trigger a negative response to the situation, hopefully it does not, and life goes on peacefully.

Moreover, the complexity of decision-making is amplified by uncertainty and ambiguity. In many situations, outcomes are very much unpredictable, and potential risks are extremely unknown. Decisions made under such conditions require a level of adaptability and resilience. Individuals must be prepared to adjust their course of action as new information emerges and be resilient in the face of unexpected challenges.

Social dynamics also contribute to the intricacy of decision-making. Interpersonal relationships, group dynamics, and societal expectations all influence the choices individuals make. Balancing personal values with societal norms and expectations can be challenging, as decisions often have ripple effects way beyond the individual. The pressure to conform or the fear of social repercussions can complicate the process of making authentic and personally meaningful decisions.

Furthermore, the long-term consequences of decisions introduce another layer of complexity. While a choice may seem advantageous in the short term, its impact over time must be sincerely be considered. This requires foresight and an ability to anticipate how decisions may unfold in the future. Evaluating potential long-term outcomes demands a comprehensive understanding of the interconnected nature of decisions and their consequences.

Additionally, cognitive biases pose a significant challenge in decision-making. Individuals may unknowingly rely on mental shortcuts and biases that can lead to suboptimal choices. Recognizing and mitigating these biases require self-awareness and a commitment to critical thinking. Overcoming cognitive biases is an ongoing process that involves continuous learning and a willingness to challenge one's own assumptions.

In the end the complexity of making the right decisions arises from the interplay of information overload, emotional influences, uncertainty, social dynamics, long-term consequences, and cognitive biases. Navigating this intricate landscape requires a combination of analytical thinking, emotional intelligence, adaptability, foresight, and a commitment to self-awareness. It is an ongoing journey that demands continuous learning and a willingness to embrace the complexities inherent in the decision-making process.

If you find a path with no obstacles, it probably doesn't lead anywhere.

—"Frank A. Clark"

If you are seeking the right path, you are already on the right path.

—"Yehunda Bergg"

SIX

20. ITEMS NEEDED FOR WALKING THE RIGHT PATH OF EFFECTIVE DECISION MAKING

Walking the right path in decision making involves following a systematic and thoughtful approach. Here are some key steps to consider while walking your path.

1. **Self-awareness:** Knowing oneself is crucial for walking the right path. It involves understanding personal values, strengths, and weaknesses. For instance, acknowledging a tendency to procrastinate allows one to take proactive measures to stay on track.

2. **Goal Setting:** Clearly defined goals provide direction. Whether it's career aspirations or personal development milestones, setting specific, measurable, achievable, relevant, and time-bound (SMART) goals helps in staying focused.

3. **Discipline:** The ability to stay committed to tasks despite challenges is essential. Disciplined individuals adhere to routines, meet deadlines, and resist distractions, fostering progress on the right path.

4. **Adaptability:** Life is dynamic, and being open to change is crucial. Adapting to new circumstances and learning from experiences ensures that setbacks become opportunities for growth.

5. **Resilience:** Resilience helps navigate obstacles without losing sight of the end goal. Overcoming failures, rejection, or criticism is part of the journey toward the right path.

6. **Empathy:** Understanding and considering others' perspectives fosters positive relationships. This emotional intelligence is vital for collaboration and maintaining ethical decisions.

7. **Continuous Learning:** The right path involves constant growth. Embracing a mindset of lifelong learning ensures that one evolves with the changing landscape, both personally and professionally.

8. **Time Management:** Effectively utilizing time is crucial. Prioritizing tasks, avoiding procrastination, and recognizing time wasters contribute to progress on the right path.

9. **Integrity:** Upholding moral and ethical principles builds trust and credibility. Making deci-

sions based on honesty and transparency is fundamental to walking the right path.

10. **Mindfulness:** Being present in the moment cultivates a deeper understanding of oneself and the surrounding environment. Mindfulness reduces stress and enhances decision-making.

11. **Gratitude:** Appreciating what one has fosters a positive mindset. Grateful individuals tend to be more resilient and better equipped to face challenges on the right path.

12. **Networking:** Building meaningful connections opens doors to opportunities. Networking allows for sharing knowledge, gaining insights, and receiving support on the journey.

13. **Financial Literacy:** Understanding financial principles is essential for making sound decisions. Budgeting, investing wisely, and avoiding debt contribute to financial stability on the right path.

14. **Health and Wellness:** Physical and mental well-being are foundational. Regular exercise, proper nutrition, and adequate sleep contribute to sustained energy and focus.

15. **Effective Communication:** Expressing ideas clearly and listening actively fosters understanding. Strong communication skills are vital for building relationships and resolving conflicts.

16. **Courage:** Taking risks and confronting fears is necessary for growth. Courageous decisions propel individuals forward on the right path, even when faced with uncertainty.

17. **Humility:** Acknowledging mistakes and seeking improvement is a sign of humility. Embracing a

humble attitude allows for continuous self-reflection and learning.

18. **Environmental Responsibility:** Acting in ways that consider the impact on the environment contributes to a sustainable and responsible life path.

19. **Balance:** Striking a balance between work, relationships, and personal time is crucial. Avoiding burnout and maintaining a healthy lifestyle are integral to staying on the right path.

20. **Vision:** Having a clear vision of the desired destination provides motivation. It serves as a guiding light, helping individuals make decisions aligned with their long-term objectives.

Let me Summarize and break down these twenty items right now.

Breakdown 1: Personal Development

Self-awareness, goal setting, and discipline are foundational aspects of personal development. Self-awareness lays the groundwork for understanding oneself, while goal setting and discipline provide the structure needed to achieve personal objectives. These three qualities work in tandem to foster individual growth and success. The more you know yourself, the more you want for yourself and the more you plan and prepare you will know what you want out of life. Preparations will make walking the path of decisions a lot easier to make the right decision.

Breakdown 2: Emotional Intelligence and Resilience Adaptability, resilience, and empathy form the core of emotional intelligence. The ability to adapt to change, bounce back from challenges, and empathize with others are crucial skills in navigating both personal and professional relationships. These qualities contribute to emotional resilience and foster a positive and supportive environment. Is the path getting clearer?

Breakdown 3: Continuous Improvement Continuous learning and time management are essential for ongoing personal and professional development. Embracing a mindset of continuous learning enables individuals to stay relevant and adapt to evolving circumstances. Effective time management is the key to maximizing productivity and ensuring a balanced approach to various life priorities. Learning, time management and development helps your decision making.

Breakdown 4: Values and Relationships Integrity, mindfulness, gratitude, and networking are interconnected elements that shape one's values and relationships. Integrity and mindfulness contribute to ethical decision-making, while gratitude fosters a positive outlook. Networking helps build meaningful connections, leveraging relationships for personal and professional growth. This will help you make the right decision for your peers as well as yourself, people are relying on you.

Breakdown 5: Holistic Well-being Financial literacy, health and wellness, effective communication, courage, humility, environmental responsibility, balance, and vision collectively contribute to holistic well-being. Financial literacy ensures sound financial decisions, while health and wellness address physical and mental well-being. Effective communication, courage, humility, environmental responsibility, balance, and vision round out a well-rounded and purposeful life.

Holistic well-being is something dear to me so let me explain why. In 2022 I was diagnosed with prostate cancer and my PSA levels were rising fast and when I say fast, I meant very fast I went from a 4.3 in May of 2022 to a 5.7 in June of 2022 and that was under a month. Cancer was coming fast I was scared and nervous, but I never told no one that. In all reality I was very frightened. My courage was gone although I just walked around smug like I wasn't bothered at all. I knew if I worried then the people around me would worry and I needed them feeling secure. I was the most Scared that I had ever been in my life, and I do not scare easily. I was procrastinating because my urologist told me that I could wait to see if it increases, or I can set up for surgery now. I was unsure what path or road to take, there goes my walk the path decision making because I was not sure. Luckily, I had a good friend that's more of a brother in my ear and he said to set that surgery up now don't let it get worse. I did just that although I was nervous. The questions about this Holistic chapter all hit me at once. Will I mentally be ok after, will I be ok to financially make sure that my family is ok if something happens to me, will I recover the right way, will my body function the same. Then the courage kicked in and I was ok. Sometimes the path is there but it can be a nervous one but I'm glad I chose the right path and today I am proud as well as thankful to say that I am Cancer free.

Each of these paragraphs highlights the interconnected nature of these qualities, emphasizing their collective impact on personal and professional decision making.

"There are no wrong turnings. Only paths we had not known we were meant to walk."

—Gavriel Kay

SEVEN

THE ULTIMATE TEST

Navigating the dichotomy between right and wrong is an age-old struggle, a profound test that transcends cultural and ethical boundaries. It is the crucible in which human character is forged, defining the essence of our morality. The ultimate test lies not just in discerning right from wrong but in the choices we make when confronted with this fundamental duality.

Choosing what is wrong often appears tempting, more exciting, offering immediate gratification or an apparent shortcut to success. The allure of the forbidden can be irresistible, pulling us into a moral quagmire where the boundaries between right and wrong blur. This path, though initially appealing, often leads to a labyrinth of consequences, challenging the very fabric of our integrity.

On the contrary, doing what is right demands resilience, structure, ethical fortitude, and a commitment to principles that stand the test of time. It requires us to rise above the allure of expediency and embrace the arduous journey of moral rectitude. Doing what is right is not always synonymous with ease; it may demand sacrifice, perseverance, and the courage to swim against the currents of societal norms. It is not easy all the time.

The ultimate test unfolds in the crucible of decision-making. Each choice, a brushstroke on the canvas of our moral identity, shapes the narrative of our character. In the face of adversity, the true mettle of our moral compass is revealed. It is during these defining moments that the distinction between right and wrong becomes palpable, and our choices echo through the corridors of time.

The consequences of choosing the wrong path are multifaceted, reaching beyond the individual to permeate relationships, communities, and societies. Wrongdoing, like a corrosive agent, erodes the trust that binds the social fabric. It leaves a trail of shattered reputations and broken bonds, casting a shadow on the very foundations of human interaction.

Conversely, doing what is right fosters a culture of trust, integrity, and collective well-being. It lays the groundwork for a harmonious coexistence, where individuals can rely on the moral uprightness of one another. Righteous actions, like seeds planted in fertile soil, yield a harvest of virtue that nourishes the collective spirit.

The ultimate test is not a singular event but a continuous journey, an ongoing narrative that unfolds in the myriad choices we make each day. It requires a commitment to self-reflection, an introspective gaze into the motives that propel our actions. Understanding the root of our decisions is paramount to navigating the intricate labyrinth of morality.

Moreover, the societal context in which the test unfolds adds another layer of complexity. Cultural norms, legal frameworks, and prevailing ideologies influence the perception of right and wrong. Negotiating these external pressures while staying true to one's moral compass is an integral aspect of the ultimate test.

In conclusion, the ultimate test of doing what's wrong versus doing what's right is a dynamic interplay of choices, consequences, and moral resilience. It is a journey that transcends individual interests, weaving the tapestry of human morality. In the crucible of decision-making, our character is shaped, and the echoes of our choices resonate far beyond the confines of the present moment. It is a test that challenges us to be architects of our moral destiny, navigating the complexities of right and wrong with wisdom, courage, and unwavering integrity.

In any moment of decision, the best thing you can do is the right thing, the next best thing is the wrong thing, and the worst thing you can do is nothing.

—Theodore Roosevelt

EIGHT

DECIDING TO MAKE THE RIGHT CHOICE

C hoosing to do the right thing is a fundamental aspect of personal and moral development. It reflects a commitment to ethical principles and values that guide one's actions. The decision to make the right choice often involves a complex interplay of internal and external factors, including one's upbringing, personal beliefs, societal norms, and the specific context of the situation.

At the core of making the right choice is the recognition of a moral compass—a set of internalized principles that serve as a guide for ethical decision-making. This moral compass is shaped by various influences, such as family, education, and cultural background. For instance, a person raised in an environment that emphasizes honesty, empathy, and compassion is likely to prioritize these values when faced with moral dilemmas.

However, the journey to making the right choice is not always straightforward. External pressures, conflicting interests, and the fear of consequences can create internal conflicts that challenge one's commitment to doing what is right. In these moments, individuals must navigate a delicate balance between their principles and the pragmatic realities of the situation.

Moreover, the concept of the "right thing" is subjective and can vary based on cultural, religious, and individual perspectives. What may be considered the right choice in one context might be viewed differently in another. This adds an additional layer of complexity to the decision-making process, requiring individuals to engage in critical reflection and consider diverse viewpoints.

In making the right choice, individuals often grapple with questions of morality, ethics, and the greater good. They may need to weigh short-term benefits against long-term consequences, and consider the impact of their actions on both themselves and others. This deliberative process requires a high level of cognitive and emotional intelligence, as well as a willingness to accept responsibility for the outcomes of one's decisions.

Taking responsibility for one's choices is a crucial aspect of doing the right thing. It involves acknowledging the consequences of one's actions and being accountable for the impact they may have on individuals and communities. This accountability is a cornerstone of ethical behavior and contributes to the development of trust and integrity in personal and professional relationships.

The decision to do the right thing is not always met with immediate rewards or recognition. In fact, individuals who choose to act ethically may face challenges, criticism, or adversity. Yet, the intrinsic satisfaction that comes from aligning one's actions with one's values often outweighs external validation. This internal fulfillment serves as a powerful motivator for continued ethical behavior and contributes to the cultivation of a strong moral character.

Additionally, doing the right thing extends beyond individual actions and encompasses a collective responsibility to promote justice, fairness, and equality in society. Individuals who are committed to ethical conduct may actively engage in efforts to address social issues, challenge systemic injustices, and advocate for positive change. This broader perspective underscores the interconnectedness of personal choices and societal well-being.

The decision to do the right thing is a multifaceted and deeply personal journey. It involves the navigation of internal and external influences, the consideration of diverse perspectives, and the willingness to take responsibility for one's actions. While the path to making ethical choices may be challenging, the rewards in terms of personal integrity, fulfillment, and contribution to a better society are invaluable. Ultimately, the choice to do the right thing is a continuous commitment to upholding ethical principles and making a positive impact on the world.

"In the space between yes and no, there is a lifetime. It's the difference between the path you walk and one you leave behind; it's the gap between who you thought you could be and who you really are; it's the legroom for the lies you will tell yourself in the future."

— Jodi Picoult, Change of Heart

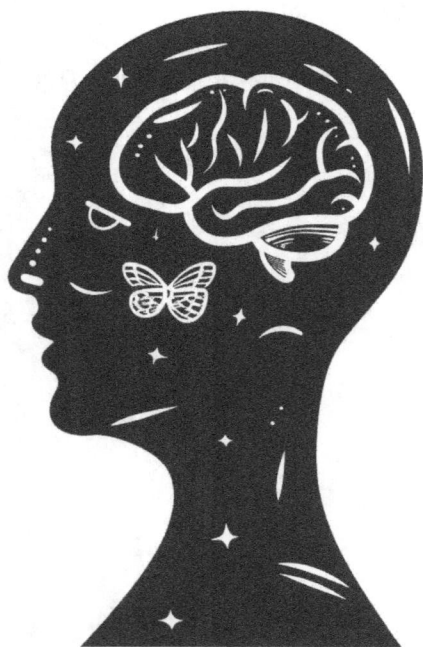

NINE

SIMPLE & EFFECTIVE DECISION MAKING

Decision-making is a complex cognitive process that we engage in daily, ranging from mundane choices to significant life-altering decisions. While some decisions are straightforward, others require a more nuanced approach. Here, we'll explore a simple yet effective framework for making decisions that can be applied to various scenarios.

1. **Define the Decision:** Clearly articulate the decision you need to make. Whether it's choosing between job offers, deciding on a weekend ac-

tivity, or making a major life choice, understanding the decision at hand is crucial.

2. **Identify Goals and Priorities:** List your goals and
   priorities related to the decision. Consider what
   matters most to you in the short and long term.
   This step helps align your decision with your
   values and aspirations.

3. **Gather Information:** Collect relevant information to make an informed choice. This may
   involve research, seeking advice, or drawing on
   past experiences. The more information you
   have, the better equipped you'll be to evaluate
   your options.

4. **Explore Alternatives:** Brainstorm different alternatives. Don't settle for the first option that
   comes to mind. Generating alternatives widens
   your perspective and increases the likelihood of
   finding the best solution.

5. **Evaluate Pros and Cons:** Assess the advantages
   and disadvantages of each alternative. Create
   a list or mental map to compare the potential
   outcomes. This process can reveal insights into
   which option aligns most closely with your goals.

6. **Consider Risks and Uncertainties:** Acknowledge potential risks and uncertainties associated with each alternative. Assess the likelihood
   and impact of these factors on the outcome.
   Being aware of potential challenges prepares
   you for contingencies.

7. **Trust Your Instincts:** Intuition can be a powerful
   guide. After considering the facts and weighing
   the options, listen to your instincts. Sometimes,

your gut feeling aligns with your subconscious understanding of the situation.

8. **Seek Advice:** Consult with trusted friends, family, or mentors. They may offer perspectives you hadn't considered and provide valuable insights based on their experiences. However, remember that the final decision is yours.

9. **Time Considerations:** Evaluate the time constraints associated with each option. Some decisions require immediate action, while others may benefit from a more deliberate, time-sensitive approach. Factor in deadlines and long-term implications.

10. **Reflect on Values:** Consider how each option aligns with your core values. A decision that resonates with your values is more likely to bring fulfillment and satisfaction in the long run.

11. **Weighted Decision Matrix:** For more complex decisions, create a weighted decision matrix. Assign weights to different criteria based on their importance and evaluate each alternative against these criteria. This structured approach adds objectivity to your decision-making process.

12. **Test with Small Steps:** If possible, test aspects of your decision on a small scale before committing to a larger course of action. This can provide insights into potential challenges and confirm the viability of your chosen path.

13. **Embrace Adaptability:** Understand that decisions may need adjustments as circumstances change. Embrace adaptability and be willing to

modify your course based on new information or evolving priorities.

14. **Decision Commitment:** Once you've made a decision, commit to it. Doubt is natural, but dwelling on it can hinder progress. Trust your judgment and focus on moving forward with confidence.

15. **Learn from Outcomes:** Regardless of the outcome, view it as an opportunity to learn. Understand what worked well and what could be improved in your decision-making process. This reflection contributes to personal growth and enhanced decision-making skills in the future.

In the end, decision-making is a dynamic process that involves careful consideration, introspection, and a willingness to adapt. By following these simple steps, you can navigate decisions with greater clarity and confidence, leading to choices that align with your goals and values.

"Sometimes you make the right decision, sometimes you make the decision right."

–Phil McGraw

"Decision making is easy when your values are clear."

–Roy Disney

TEN

THE RELIEF OF MAKING THE RIGHT DECISIONS

Making the right choices in life can bring a profound sense of relief. These decisions, whether big or small, often lead to positive outcomes and a sense of fulfillment. One aspect of this relief is the assurance that comes with knowing you've taken a path aligned with your values and goals. It provides a sense of purpose and direction, contributing to long-term happiness. The assurance that your decisions align with your values and aspirations creates a harmonious internal landscape, fostering a positive and empowering mindset. This relief stems from the knowledge that each choice is a step forward on the path of personal growth and fulfillment. As you navigate life's crossroads, the satisfaction derived from making sound decisions resonates deeply within, establishing a foundation for confidence and resilience. The relief of right choices is not merely a fleeting emotion; it forms the bedrock of a life well-lived, a mosaic of purposeful actions and their corresponding positive consequences.

Another dimension of relief in making right choices is the avoidance of potential negative consequences. Correct decisions can prevent regrets, guilt, or the burden of dealing with undesirable outcomes. This relief stems from the understanding that your choices have led to favorable results, sparing you from unnecessary stress and hardship.

Moreover, making right choices often fosters personal growth. The relief comes not only from the immediate positive outcomes but also from the long-term development and improvement in various aspects of life. These choices become stepping stones towards a better version of yourself, cultivating self-confidence and a positive self-image.

The relief is not only internal but extends to the way others perceive you. Right choices can enhance your reputation and relationships, fostering trust and respect from those around you. The sense of relief arises from the acknowledgment and appreciation of your decision-making skills, creating a positive social environment.

Furthermore, making right choices can lead to a more stable and secure future. Whether it's in terms of career, finances, or relationships, the relief comes from knowing that your decisions have contributed to building a foundation for a prosperous and sustainable life. This foresight provides a sense of security and peace of mind.

Lastly, the relief of making the right choices often manifests in improved overall well-being. Mental and emotional health can benefit from the reduced stress and anxiety that stem from poor decisions. The sense of relief becomes a catalyst for a positive feedback loop, encouraging a mindset of proactive decision-making and resilience in the face of challenges.

In conclusion, the relief of making the right choices goes beyond immediate gratification. It encompasses a holistic sense of well-being, personal growth, and positive impact on various aspects of life.

The assurance, avoidance of negative consequences, personal development, enhanced relationships, future stability, and improved well-being collectively contribute to the profound relief that accompanies the art of making right choices. With the right choices we all realize that We Can not serve two master's At all. Please choose the master that you desire to serve correctly!

Are you stuck trying to unstick yourself and make the right choices in life? What steps does it take to be effective in your decision making? Are you curious as to how to finally get started? How to get your mindset elevating to your highest mental capacity? Well, let this book guide you into taking the 1st leap into Decision freedom. Before one can obtain success, one has to believe it, live it and challenge ourselves to be effective on what we decide. Let this book open up your mindset to show you that" You can't Serve 2 masters and how to get to the right decision"."

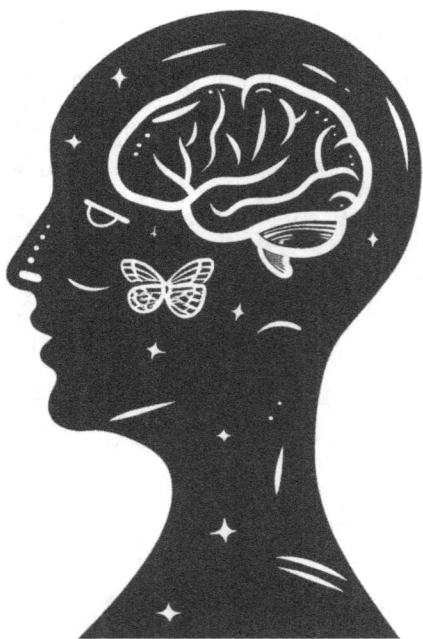

ABOUT THE AUTHOR

Davielier Turner is an established Real Estate Broker, Instructor, Real Estate Coach & a Success coach in the New Jersey area that has been flipping real estate and understand the teaching of a positive mindset for over 20+ years. He is also part owner of Pinnacle Real Estate Group located in Jersey City Nj and the sole owner of B.C Enterprises, a company that specializes in property redevelopment in Urban Neighborhoods.

www.ingramcontent.com/pod-product-compliance
Lightning Source LLC
La Vergne TN
LVHW051810080426
835513LV00017B/1897